To my kids:

Thanks for not sucking.

To the reader:

[Insert what you'd like to hear about yourself]

Coffee and Skin

O' pitter A flutter A patter O' flutter

O' pitter does my heart pump, pump-
A flutter and my throat glump, glump.

For beauty rays as sunshine lays
light upon your skin-
Your peach-tree smile serenades
my eyes, wherein
my gaze settles for a while.

Your sweet-scent hair is
dripping silk in worlds of
coarse frayed twine,
lighter here and darker there-
the brown strands' force
stops time.

Lips for miles and pink-blushed smiles
blur the side-seen world-
Your love-dunked gaze reconciles
my mind, unfurled.
My trepidation
    Uh. waits.

Your soft-touch skin is
freckled with spots of stars-
All shine,
mapping out a finger-trace
to reach them all
       in time.

A patter does my heart bump, bump-
O' flutter and my chest jump, jump.

Pirate Carnival

My lungs expand with trepidation,
But you
          Pop them. Like balloons.

Lips are dry,
And fingertips
          Smooth the edges down.

Hair in strands
Of sweet sensation,
          I clutch them like doubloons.

Feed me with your magic thoughts,
Soak me in your think,
Touch me with your fingers crossed
And tip me, tip me like your drink.

Silver Skin

I sip-sip the air and it drip-drips
             my blush away.
Slowly tip-tip the ripping grip 'til
        it fades and lets
                 our fingers sway-
Your skin smooth like silver.
Your lips of pilfered longing.
And us sitting
         in
                 the rain.

Emptied and warm enough
my beating
         heart-beat fades
as though I'm
         running out of pumps-
Never were you mine.
The thunks and glunks and
         throat-sunk lumps
I should have heard
         have been passive 'til this time.

Early Morning Walk

Wring me dry of sleep.
Stir me in your coffee mug
and let me bask in post-dream drug-
For my eyes do seek
two green drops of morning sun.

Below those drops pose two pink lips.
I'd reach across with fingertips
And
Just
Touch
a morning with you.

Tell me how you've slept,
Teach me who you are
and where your dreams are kept
so slowly
we'll go
Far.

Walk across the grassy dew,
Although it chills you as it may-
Whilst savoring your infant day
know my mind was thoughts of you.

Wake yourself as kisses could
because, if there, I would.

Chewing on Sunset Skies

A pink-eyed field of grassy fingers
Swimming with the wind ties my
Mind in a sky-stitched haze of
Pulled-apart purple like
Fair cotton candy
Sticking to
You
As though
It'd like to be left
Between your teeth but
The webbed strands of sugar-sky
Melt as quickly as the sunset sinks
And a shadow chews on green fingers.

Rainfall Calm

Your fingers feel like common sense,
Your lips are where I roam-
Your eyes in mine are soft-intense.
They seem to take me home.

The comfort sits within me,
Oh, how you do refill-
The grabby ghost of heartbeats boast
        a thump amidst the still.

Calmness spills around us-
It overflows like hand-dug sand
after waning waves.
You have become my truss-
Your anchor digs into my skin
        and sturdiness it paves.

Your hair is like a rainfall,
My fingers wet and running through-
My heart is yours to call
once I send my lips dripping down to you.

O' comfort rest upon my left

O' comfort rest upon my left
And lead me not awry,
The trembling portion of my mind
Seems clearer than the sky.
I find no doubt, moats be drought
And crunchy to the feet-
Trek across the barren bound
And find me here to meet.

My chest internal beats are heavy
Yet the pace is smooth and slight-
My ribs construct a useless levee
As fear is shallow, weak and light.

I find in mind my thoughts are strewn
Yet filled with stars and you-
Wrap your hand, and fingers too,
Then we'll float us to the moon.

Clouds of Sheets

Knee high waves amongst a comfort sea
        bleed immobility.
A single seam to cast but where, I ask,
Is where I wish to be?
An edge of light and backlit skies
        are trapped outside,
Behind true blinds
        a moonlight shines somewhere.

An empty hand, likely soft and welcome,
Reaches through the crash
And sits behind to catch the flash.

A southern swirl of ocean,
Your accent in the air-
Eyes across a white-lined bed
Where in time I'll find instead
Your smile,
        wild, warm and fair.
Pillows rest beneath you,
They smell of long sunsets-
As if the sun had slowed itself
Admiring the view.

Traipse across the warming clouds
Fingertips in-hand,
There's a host of mellow sounds
Which flow 'neath cotton-sands.

November 2013

She was crying and screaming. I rounded the steps, shielded by the half-wall separating the stairs from the room stationed above the garage. "Hey, I'm not sure exactly what you need but I'm here."

       I looked around the room in its own disarray. Toys were scattered, there was another large hole in the drywall I'd have to fix. The carpeted room was snowed over by shredded pages. Spines and backs ached from being thrown against the wall. Books unread, books read twice, unceremoniously launched as my feet began creaking up the steps. Her rage changed direction when I became available, which seemed to be her goal. As history suggests, damage is caused to incite. Until now, I'd wait it out and just spend the night cleaning before heading into work the next morning but as I heard the books being ripped, it needed to stop sooner than usual.

       I approached her with what was left of my empathy, pretty understanding of where this was going. She stopped screaming and crying but knelt there next to the torn books. She positioned herself to be in a place of dominance, now she'd see if I could read her mind.

       My feet trekked, kneeling beside her and my arms began to hug her. She pushed me away. Her dark green eyes wet with anger. Light coffee-stained skin and straight brown hair were fire. "You can't just hug me without saying anything" she burned into me. I replied, trying my best to hide the distaste for another night, "Oh, I'm sorry, I just thought-" she stopped me. "Thought, of course you thought. You always think and never do. Stop thinking and just do things, that's all I want from this, it'll fix everything." I let her finish, paused and said, "Like how I just hugged you instead of taking time to figure out the right thing to do?" She began to open her mouth to spit acid. I didn't give her the chance and continued "Look, I'm trying here. I've tried leaving you alone when you cry, I've tried being there with you and holding you, I've tried being near you and letting you control the situation. Just tell me what you need me to do and I'll do it and we can stop this."

Precipitation

Greyblackclouds puffaround ominousandheavy
likeAmindspillingover drippingdownsteady
Whereraindrops wouldbe hardertoavoid. Though,
Itmayjust be timetoletfall whatIknow.

W   ic   d   o   s   ’ t

   h   h   e   n

         S   e   m
                e

T   o   b   l   h a

         e   A   l   t   t

M   u   h   a   l

      c   t   a   l.

Melatonin Morning

Trudging amongst the trees through drowsy scenes
I found my knees in cold-kissed, green-slicked waters.
In breath I'll hold to keep the sun so gold as it clears the crystal blues.
If cues could breach my mind, I'd have seen the wide-gaped submarine
          disguised as a city lined with manta ray skin.
As its jaws panned side to side, this sweet foreign hand in time
Grasped me in my affectioned surprise. I thought,
Then thanked this single serving friend with Spanish eyes (His not mine).

Past perplexed to onward tracks and sure enough that way,
This single train still remained without a pilot's guiding sway.
I learned (and guessed) this awkward mess, the little lurching sleigh,
I pulled it forward, coal in gear, towards the tiny house of gray.

I trekked in snowy air through somber dark dismay,
Without a moon the wolves howled empty, panting in the back.
The stars gave up their light to pull me without a sky to track,
Shiver up the mountain, huddled I shake and stay.
If I, for once, can find this resting place,
I, for once, will see me face to face.

There's still a beast to find which digs the treasure's grave,
And people there between me with pages meant to save-
This off lit little village kept me from my honest,
It kept me far away,
As some admonish most any other day.
I'll dream again and get there, find my treasure's keep.
I'll dream until it's not a dream and finally fulfill-
I'll find every bit within me; I'll just dream until.

If you were actually here.

For the red that's wrapped in sparkle tape,
The filled chocolates and cards heart-shaped-
I admit none of such will do, as I, for you
May not.
The notes I'd hide, sweet potatoes french-fried,
Are not around this time, but keep in mind,
Inside my head my kisses slide
Down your cheeks and across your lips.
My fingertip sips your salt-tendered skin.
Your room-lit green eyes and soft dimpled-smile
Shook my heart for a little while,
It beeped and beeped out and in,
Beeped until my chest caved in.

I woke inside my dream all wired,
Heart stopped, tangled and numbly tired.
And you were there,
I could trace the freckles you hid from me,
I could see all we'd ever be
And I knew through all eternity that you'd know it's me.
I'd hold your hand, wrap your lips in mine
And watch the sand drip an hourglass spine-
When just before the time ran out
I'd flip it because time without you is just
Without.

Crisping Stream

There was a sun that used to set,
       It'd dip dip dip until it'd sit-
But that was 'fore you two met
       And hence the sky keeps lovely lit.
Trees of green with leaves to fall
       Would wrap the wind in splendor-
Paint the air in colors all
       But here abscission won't render.

Here's to you, unchanging too,
       your eyes
       your lips
       and beauty wisps.
Cascading steps of water view-
       it tries
       it slips
       and even crisps.
Though naught compared to you.

The creek runs wet where motion stays,
With rocks stretching out to see-
Cotton clouds pause to gaze
       and here we all agree:

Gold-brown waves of summer shades,
       southern lips of playful fire-
Sun-touched skin with pinkish fades
       and my eyes will never tire.

January 2014

"Oh, there's plenty left to destroy, I can do this all night until you stop me."

 She was right, in a way, I found out. After patching up golf club drives in the wall, spackling knife holes down the hallway, there was always something else.

 "I'm not going to sit up here and do this with you again. If I'm not here, you break everything. If I'm here, you break everything and blame it on me, and then it just gets worse, and you get crazy violent. You need to stop this or I'm going to call the police again-"

 Her voice smoothly shifted to an intense paranoid rage in a practiced way "Don't you dare call the police again, they'll put me in the hospital and abuse me."

 "Maybe if you didn't do crazy shit they wouldn't think you were crazy. I'm going back downstairs, me being up here just makes you worse so you need to deal with it on your own or let me know when you want to talk. I'm going to go downstairs, hopefully the kids are still sleeping."

My empathy dried up. Her destroying the white Ibanez was dehydrating, everything felt gone. Everything else she had done seemed meaningless compared to that. I walked down the stairs, books smashing around my head as I did. Slamming the door I thought: "I don't really want to fix all of that drywall. And I'll have to paint it too, might as well just repaint the entire room."

Where are my minds.

There used to be space for you between Keats and Poe
but now there's dust and sweet merlot dripping down real low.
I think there was a picture too, some grass we hadn't touched-
then that fell off the shelf and burned as it was clutched.

I look around to see what else used to be misplaced,
your shoes aground, all around and often oddly spaced.
I'd find through spite a high heel right where it shouldn't be,
I'd stumble each and every night if you'd return to me.

The knives and forks are dulling now as they rest askew,
our spoons still sit deeply snug as if they might find you.
The drip-drip sink grows ever loud as it inner aches,
my brain pounds and pounds like echoes in the lakes.

I find myself by myself sitting on the floor,
for you and me there used to be the lofty French amour-
but now there's wicked gravity to bounce around my bones-
it's all pressed back, as powder rapped, shattering my stones.

Reeks of Metamorphosis

Hallow be thy silver bar,
In place of pills or sweetened tar-
The body-wreck and gentle sway
Of handled bells and dumbbell play.
The rubber plates or metaled shapes
Heal mind and soul as farmer traipse.

Though I wake a chagrined channel-
with summer aching sweat,
I owe myself a swift dismantle
and another heavy set.

Early mid-life crisis

Eat my chest off the mirr'r as perplexion reflects
          an image I can hide in angles and dim lights.
My skin concedes its err'red ways,
The tidal of my hair flows in praise
          and lip-shaped bruises deepen heart-beat bites.

Touch the glass with your fingertip judgement
          to smudge me down the middle.
Oil on your fingerprints in appreciative haste
so I can find
          the best of me
                    for you to lip-stick taste
From all my camera's fiddle.

Swipe away the glare and dim my lights some more,
          Filter out the self-affection low beneath the floor.
And, though I crave myself in every inch to pour-
          It's not exactly me, what I'm looking for.

August 2026

 "Well, I got you a pretty sweet coffee cup. It'll keep your coffee hot for almost the whole day so you don't have to swig tepid brew through your undealt-with teenage angst."

"I appreciate the thought, but I don't mind the tepid as much as you think." The microwave door shut and a few buttons beeped. "Besides, how did you find something that fit my personality? How am I supposed to show swagger with these child-bearing hips if I'm holstering a poorly chosen chalice?"

"Dad," she started, "You'd struggle in quarter-inch heels. You don't sashay as well as you think you do and we both know your personality is 'Does it hold coffee? Because that'll do.'"

"Where do you think you get your femininity from?" I pointed to a few chest hairs gasping for air near my collar.

"YouTube. And Google. I don't even understand what this conversation is about anymore, you have 12 of the same shirt-"

"They came in a bag" I cut her off.

"Right." Her sage green eyes rolled and she shook her head from side to side. "You don't even pretend to find matching socks anymore."

"I aint a part of your system." Came out automatically.

"And your watch doesn't even have the little fucking band that keeps the tail from flopping around."

"It's weird that it still tells me the time, though."

"It's green." She stated.

"How do you know what color it is if it's not there? Pretty sure it was black."

"No, you leathered ass-hat. The cup is green."

I'd been beaten. I remember feeling my eyes moisten and the tips of my mouth curling up ever-so-slightly, but I pursed them to hide the smile.

"I do like green."

Emny stepped to her room, the floor creaking down the hall to a quick shuffle through a bag. I heard the floor returning with a hint of excitement as my daughter handed me a perfectly ounced two-piece insulating caffeine habitat.

Crunchy Couch

On a couch of lost cherry stems
are smudged fingerprints and pushed-in bits
of crushed-up chips and whate'r fits.
Unpopped kernels of cartoon lights
scratch the Holy pajamas of
Staying Up All Night-
A most welcome itch.

Concave habits curved into fabric
snuggle crawled upon and felled upon
dirty cherub antics.
And as that dirt seeps
just so it can be dredged
up in fingertip heaps-
some crusty, crispy clump stays wedged
just out of reasonable reach.

And, though, I could stretch so low
it's just as well
for I've heard that next
week can easily house the clean I seek.
So stay, cinnamon-sweet cartel,
          And soak
in another wait bestowed.

August 2026 pt.2

I turn the cup around in my hands, toss it left to right. The silver interior lining was polished in a way that screamed in puffs as I blew hot air into it, checking the fogging properties. I don't really know what that means but I enjoy how clear the breath is, and wipe the cloud away with a smudgy, oily finger.

The outer green is solid, vibrant, and dark. It is as though pastel green had been trampled by a forest and then smoothed. The textured micro-bumps are comfort sized, riding the length top to bottom. Etched near the top where the to-be coffee container widens to a natural not-for-cupholders size, is a peculiar heart. As though the back of a knife blade scraped into a memory, the heart had four limbs: Single-line legs with off-angled feet and two matching arms. In the middle of the heart were two dots, roughly spaced to fit a non-existent nose that rested precariously over a smile only a child would understand. My right thumb runs across the tiny crevices to measure their depth and I silence the intruding microwave with my left hand, opening the door.

Without words or sound, I pour the steaming brew into my new gift, listening to it fill as the pitch rises near the top. Watching it for a few seconds, heat escapes but I swept it with the lid, feeling that for now, at least, there was no heat running away. Everything I cared about was in that cup. Everything I cared about and loved was everywhere, different parts of the country, different parts of the world, and every bit of it was being temporarily contained by that lid.

Every day there's a morning.

Quench me with your bitter warmth

                  as I am all

       but lost;

Gale me 'gainst the wave henceforth

And right my dinghy tossed-

The cloud of groggy weighs me down

I need your

           brewing

              bean,

         Waft and swirl

      you slowly 'round

     to yield me

        your caffeine.

March 2027

I sipped off and on as I walked to the truck. The old paint was dusty in a way
that added texture to the simple silver.

The tires were fatigued as indicated by their male pattern baldness, they sunk
and sliced out small love handles across the flat road. The over-used tailgate
still thudded with provocative interest, one of those psychological selling
points. The seats, though capable of both heating and cooling to either
individual's taste, suffered from an imbalance of loneliness. The driver's worn
leather creaked in taught, familiar motions as I stepped up and sat in.
Looking at the full cup holders with habitual dismay, grabbed a mostly empty
mug and

dumped the remnants out the door before gently tossing it onto the
passenger floorboard.

The Last October

Sweet silver lines the sky
whilst grey turnt greyer sucks the night
'til black turns a cold, cold moon shy.
Then as though to let me near
a high gust blows, and spots appear-
The clouds disperse the eerie sight
and all grounded chin up to peer.

In this dark cast overhead lie
spots of pin-pricked dots of i's
that make my bones sick.
As they click 'gainst each other
and pop as stars are counted one by one
the humbling causes my 'ternal wonder
(And aged arthritis aches)
to pain and logic blunder.

For years and years they shine so loud,
Bright and stagnant we glide 'round-
I've come so gray 'gainst their shine,
Those stars, who once were mine.

I toil and wreck as though I've slept
away any self that I had saved.
It doesn't weigh itself, a past depraved,
as the scale cannot hang
all the heavies that I've kept.

Though I lie 'neath a counted sky-
There are those I knew who don't.
The little cherubs who'd look but won't
'cause they can't from where they lie.

For years and years they shine so loud,
Bright and stagnant we glide 'round-
I've come so gray 'gainst their shine,
Those stars, who once were mine.

The calendar is a lie.

My couch is the Venn diagram overlap when I look at the wall and the floor. It
has both support and something flat, so two of my favorite things.
Overgrown dust is fingering its way out from under the couch and if it gets
any broachier, I'll have to sweep it up. Mounted TV wires hang like still-drying
umbilical cords and the bread-bag twist-ties that bundle them close make me
smile. I'm not sure why they're bundled. Each cable is obviously a cable
against the obvious white wall, being grouped together doesn't change how
many there are or where they need to go.

Every day since.

My face smells gray.
The slow opaque skin bleeds flavor trimmed
in sugar-laced dismay
as sweet-sweet green eyes dim,
Blink, blink then stay.

My mind is slow.
It used to be in misery I'd sink and curl away
but here in final throe,
While the sun sinks away the day,
I breathe then blow, in and blow.

My skin is calm.
The pores that sink have begun to show
how clammy is my palm,
I feel no bumps where wind and snow
itch surely as a bomb.

My eyes are blind.
The color-laden mini-pixels blacken out,
Which triggers fear to stay-
As I slip and stagger now
I turn colorless and grey.

October. Every October now.

Sweet liquor of fluid life found its way to me-
But I'll churn and scrape and chew
until it's solid, knotted negativity.

A metal guard protects from squeeze
while my scented tongue detects-
If you find yourself inside my chest
it's not for what you'd please.
Come through the right and jump around
between the teeth and nails,
It's up to me you see-
I'll filter out your thoughtless mind
and all your hazardry.

The bones and teeth and Ca spurs
developed years ago,
the head is new, the tumor too,
to make me hard to eat.
I've been chewed up and spit out
becoming my own doubt.
But here I am (Though chances small)
to receive my share of euphory.
Pour your life down my throat
        one
        second
        at
        a
        time
and if for you my defense shows
to rest its tired head-
I'll begin to tell you what it's like
to see while being dead.

This is me now

I used to think when I had felt that loss was misery,
But time has passed since I've held last
a hope that could be cast.

I had found in you a sweet perfume along the wicked mire,
So stick with you, my bedside shrew,
I will 'til we expire.

Hold me high through your fogged-eyes as shallow as I dig,
The sweets stay cold, 'lest they mold-
As covered in dirt and sprig.

My heart would beat but now it churns salty, gritty fire-
There's room for you inside me,
Pooling in my ire.

Round my curve

Round the curve and down the road
between the yellow trees
Groans an early morning wood-creaked floor
beneath two old worn knees.
The caffeine drips black like gold,
         the brittle mug burns arthritic fingertips
with exhausted fire slipping through his lips.

Another day past mid-old age to barter meagre wage-
Is just enough to tip-toe through
with kids to meet the template.
Matches flare 'gainst tobacco stick to move another inch-
To reach that cooling brew
and think of thoughts less desperate.

His recent daughter checks his sun-quenched ears
and sees his leathered neck,
His shoulder's torn and skin brown-spotted
as he eases down the deck.

His drive away towards heavy light
where roads would still be paved,

Allows his mind to dry-

He sinks and sinks in sunken sight
tired, drunk and shaved.
He sighs a deep and dismal breath,
Contrasts the yellow sun-
Swirls around the coffee's death
and reaches for the gun.

Just, Read.

Read me 'neath the willow wisps,
The curly drab-green fingertips,
How they stretch the wind out long-
They beckon soft and longingly
To touch the ink-dried song.

Hide me in your memory,
With pages writ all wrong,
Fire me near four-fifty
And ban me with the rest-
They fear that I will damage you
But still I'll beat your chest.
Lick me salty with the ocean,
Some east-bound low-end knots,
Turn my page with sandy tips
And thumb my curving motion-
Pink tongue 'twixt sun-kissed lips
To wet my corner thoughts.

Sound me to your children,
Seed what they can find-
And reach through their open ears
To plant me in their mind.